ANTARCTIC ICE

Jim Mastro and Norbert Wu

photographs by Norbert Wu

Henry Holt and Company · New York

To my son, Kylan, who loves penguins and seals already —J. M.

To my diving buddies and crew in Antarctica, for their hard work and sense of humor: Beez Bohner, Peter Brueggeman, Dug Coons, Andy Day, Christian McDonald, Doug Quin, Rob Robbins, DJ Roller, and Dale Stokes —N. W.

Norbert Wu's work in Antarctica was supported by the National Science Foundation's (NSF) Antarctic Artists and Writers Program in 1997, 1999, and 2000.

Henry Holt and Company, LLC, *Publishers since 1866*
115 West 18th Street, New York, New York 10011
www.henryholt.com

Henry Holt is a registered trademark of Henry Holt and Company, LLC
Text copyright © 2003 by Jim Mastro and Norbert Wu
Photographs copyright © 2003 by Norbert Wu
All rights reserved. Distributed in Canada by H. B. Fenn and Company Ltd.

Library of Congress Cataloging-in-Publication Data
Mastro, Jim. Antarctic ice / story by Jim Mastro and Norbert Wu;
photographs by Norbert Wu.
Summary: Photographs and text describe the varied animal life on the coldest
continent, focusing on the Adélie penguin, Weddell seal, and Orca whale.
1. Zoology—Antarctica—Juvenile literature. [1. Zoology—Antarctica.] I. Wu,
Norbert, ill. II. Title.   QL106 .M37 2003   591.98'9—dc21   2002012745
ISBN 0-8050-6517-2 / First Edition—2003 / Designed by Donna Mark
Printed in the United States of America on acid-free paper. ∞
10 9 8 7 6 5 4 3 2 1

Antarctica is the coldest place on earth. Most of the mountains and valleys are permanently buried under a deep layer of ice. In winter, even the surface of the ocean freezes. There are no waves. Nothing moves except the wind.

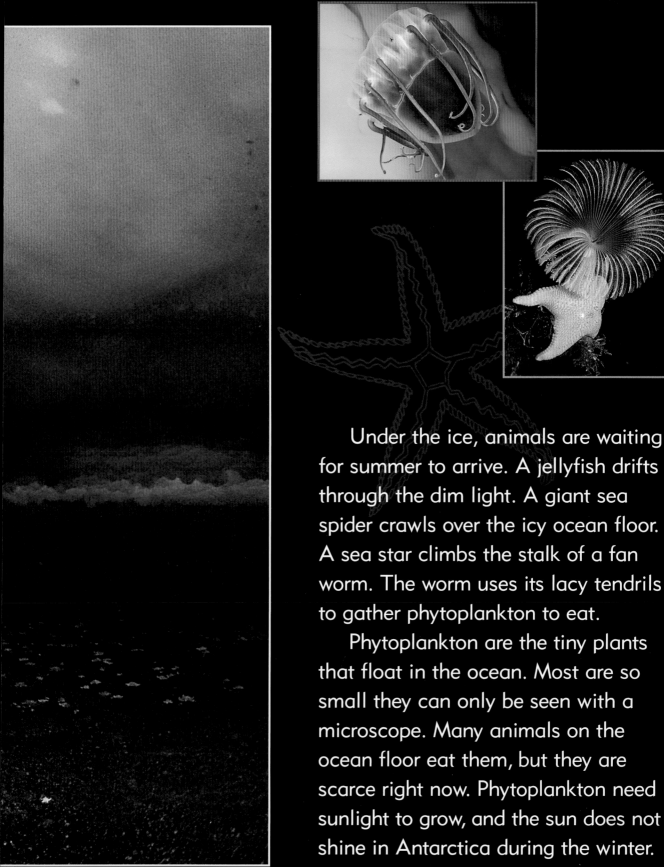

Under the ice, animals are waiting for summer to arrive. A jellyfish drifts through the dim light. A giant sea spider crawls over the icy ocean floor. A sea star climbs the stalk of a fan worm. The worm uses its lacy tendrils to gather phytoplankton to eat.

Phytoplankton are the tiny plants that float in the ocean. Most are so small they can only be seen with a microscope. Many animals on the ocean floor eat them, but they are scarce right now. Phytoplankton need sunlight to grow, and the sun does not shine in Antarctica during the winter.

Weddell seals are waiting for summer, too. They spend most of their lives under the ice, hunting for food. Sometimes they even sleep there. They find cracks in the surface and stick their noses out to breathe. The frozen sea protects the seals from the cold winter wind.

The ice shelters other animals as well. A fish uses a small hole for a home. Here he is safe from the seals who want to eat him. Simple plants called algae also live in the ice, but they are still too small to see. Just like the phytoplankton, they need the long, bright days of summer so they can grow.

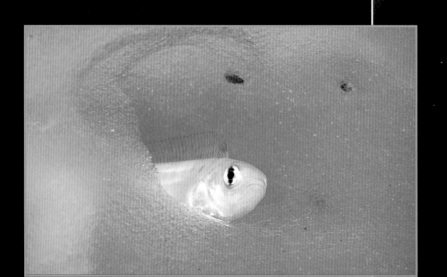

The sun returns from its long absence. Each day it rises higher in the sky and shines longer. Soon it is light all the time. There is no night at all. Summer has arrived in Antarctica, but it is still cold enough to keep the ocean's surface frozen.

A mother Weddell seal finds a crack in the ice and pulls herself out of the water. She inches across the frozen surface like a caterpillar. It is time for her to have a baby. The solid ice gives her a safe place to do it. When the pup arrives, he has a coat of thick fur to keep him warm.

Like the Weddell seals, emperor penguins have their babies on the sea ice. In the middle of winter, the mother penguin laid one egg. The father quickly placed it on his feet and covered it with a warm flap of skin. When the egg hatched, the baby emperor had her own movable nest. Now it is summer, and like the other chicks she has grown too big to sit on her father's feet.

An Orca whale swims over. Its breathing is very loud. *Whoosh!* The penguins can hear it from far away. The whale moves along the edge of the ice, looking for food. He can't squeeze through cracks like the Weddell seals, so he must stay near open water. Big fish live deep under the ice, and the whale hunts them. Sometimes the whale will eat seals, too, but this time they are safely out of reach on the ice.

After several days of swimming south from his winter home, an Adélie penguin arrives at the ice edge. He is on his way to the rookery, the place where he and his mate will raise their chicks. The small penguin can take only short steps, so it is a long walk for him.

At last he reaches the rookery. It is on a low hill that has no ice. The male must hurry to build his nest of stones before the female arrives. There aren't many stones around, so sometimes he sneaks over and steals one from his neighbor.

Summer is a very busy time under the ice, too. The tiny algae grow fast in the bright sun and form a brown film on the bottom of the ice. This is the food many animals have been waiting for. Urchins, sea stars, and little creatures called amphipods and krill eat the algae. Fish eat the amphipods and krill, and seals and penguins eat the fish. (Penguins eat krill, too.)

Back on land, the female Adélie penguin arrives at the rookery. To get reacquainted, the penguins sing to each other and wiggle their flippers. The female lays two eggs, then she leaves again. Laying has made her very hungry. She has to go back to the ocean to eat. Off she goes on her long walk over the ice. The male sits on the eggs and keeps them warm.

The emperor chick gets bigger as summer goes on. When her parents leave to go fishing, she joins the other chicks, who have formed a group called a crèche.

The baby emperors are still too young to swim. Without ice to stand on, they wouldn't survive. The parents come back every couple of days with their stomachs full of fish, squid, and krill. They pass some of this partially digested food into the hungry chick's mouth.

The baby Weddell seal has gotten bigger, too. His mother has decided it is time for him to learn to swim. The two of them slip through a crack into the water. The mother stays very close to protect her pup.

The sea ice softens and begins to melt in the summer sun. Large pieces break off from the edge. More and more of the sea is uncovered. The ice algae are released and drift down to the ocean floor. Sponges and other marine animals sift them out of the water to eat. Everyone depends on the algae, and the algae depend on the ice.

The female Adélie doesn't have quite as far to walk when she returns to the rookery. She replaces the father, who goes off to eat. While he is away, the eggs hatch. The two fuzzy chicks are hungry. Just like the emperor penguin parents, the mother Adélie spits up partially digested food into each chick's mouth.

The cracks in the ice grow bigger. The Weddell seal pup spends more time in the water. He is learning to hold his breath for a long time so he can dive like his mother to find fish. Now that the ice is breaking up, the fish are running out of places to hide.

The animals on the bottom enjoy all the food raining down from the surface. As the ice breaks up, more algae fall down where they can reach it. The bright sun has made lots of phytoplankton grow in the water, and some of this drifts down to the sea floor as well. Even animals that don't eat algae and phytoplankton have a feast. Some sea stars find a nice, juicy urchin to eat.

The brief summer draws to an end. Most of the sea ice has melted. The emperor penguin chicks must quickly learn how to swim before it disappears entirely. The Adélie penguins can now just walk to the shore and jump in.

The sun dips lower in the sky. It is getting colder. The emperor chicks begin swimming north, where they will spend the winter. Once the Adélie chicks grow adult feathers, they too will dive into the ocean and swim north. In just a few days, the nests are empty.

All too soon, the short summer is over. The Orcas and Weddell seal pups have gone north for the winter, but some of the adult Weddell seals have stayed behind. They are used to living in the ice.

Winter arrives quickly in Antarctica. The ocean's surface begins to freeze again. Before long, nothing moves but the wind. Everything is waiting for summer to return once more.